The Mad, Mad, Mad World of Salvador Dalí

Prestel

How do you become a superstar?

When he was just a little boy of eight, Salvador Dalí made an art studio for himself where he could do some painting. It was up in the attic of his parents' house in the Spanish town of Figueras. Instead of reading children's books and comics, he read books about art history. Six years later, when he was in his teens, he was showing his own paintings in an art exhibition. In time, Dalí was to become one of the most famous and successful artists of the twentieth century. He was always ready to surprise the world with amazing new ideas—he really was a superstar in the art world.

When he was grown-up, Salvador Dalí often painted things that had happened or that he remembered from his child-hood. The trees in the painting on the right are the ones he used to see as a boy when he looked out of his classroom window. The tower behind them looks like the mill on the country estate where Dalí once went for a holiday after taking his entrance exam to secondary school. And who is the painter sitting in front of the easel at the bottom of the picture? Is it Dalí himself, perhaps? No, not at all. It is an artist Dalí liked very much. His name is Jan Vermeer van Delft and he lived in Holland over four hundred years ago. Dalí is in the picture, too. He is the little boy in the sailor suit with his nanny sitting next to him.

2

Enigmatic Elements in the Landscape, 1934

Is this a monster or something in a dream?

This enormous, heavy face, propped up on crutches, looks a bit like the film director Luis Buñuel who was a friend of Dalí's. The two of them made a couple of films together that caused quite a stir in their day. But the face also looks like a curiously formed rock at Cape Creus in the south of Spain which Dalí used to explore during his holidays as a boy.

Dalí portrays sleep as a monster which would lose its balance without the crutches. He wrote that if just one of the crutches were to be taken away, the giant would wake up and the boat in the dream scene would disappear immediately. Perhaps the same would also happen to the dog which Dalí might have played with as a child. Dalí went on to explain that crutches often give way and then we topple over. Perhaps you have had this feeling too— just before you fall asleep, you dream that you are tumbling and then suddenly wake up with a jerk!

For Dalí, sleep was part of his work as a painter. By examining his dreams he hoped to find new ideas and images which he would never have thought of while awake.

Sleep, 1937

What goes on inside our heads?

The burning giraffe

What could be hidden in the drawers of this tall woman's body? What are her secret desires, dreams and fears? Salvador Dalí thought that we all have lots of secret compartments inside us. He was a great admirer of Sigmund Freud, an Austrian professor who went to live in London. Freud became famous for his way at looking into how our minds work—or the subconscious, as it is properly called. He found out that we can see into our minds by looking at the dreams we have which don't seem to make any sense, by studying the odd mistakes we make when we speak or by examining things that we imagine even though we know that they cannot be possible.

Portrait of Sigmund Freud, 1938

The image of the burning giraffe could have been taken from one of Dalí's bad dreams. However, another artist, René Magritte, who had been painting pictures of burning trumpets and keys just a little earlier, complained that Dalí was copying his ideas. Both artists belonged to an international group of painters called the Surrealists who were not happy with simply painting what they saw. Instead, they turned their attention inwards and tried to paint the world as they saw it in their own heads and dreams

The Burning Giraffe, 1936/37

The melting clocks

Why are there strange clocks on the beach?

Dalí let us in on a secret. One evening he was too tired to go out to the cinema with his wife and friends. He had just eaten some very good Camembert that had gone all soft and runny and couldn't stop thinking about this gooey cheese. He went back into his studio for one last look at the picture he was painting before calling it a day. The background, showing the beach near his hometown Port Lligat, was already finished, but the foreground was empty—it needed something exciting in it.

The Persistence of Memory, 1931

Dalí was just about to go to bed when he had a brilliant idea. Melting clocks were the answer! In spite of his headache he started painting right away. By the time his wife came back home two hours later, he had already finished the painting.

This became one of Dalí's most famous pictures—a picture that shows us that time never stands still.

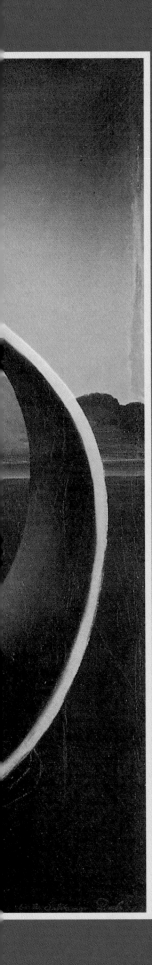

Strange encounters

Dalí was strangely fascinated by fried eggs. He liked to imagine two of them next to each other so that they looked like a pair of eyes—perhaps the eyes of his wife, Gala, who with her penetrating stare used to read cards and look into the future. Just as eyes and fried eggs are similar in shape, so too are the snail and the telephone receiver in this painting.

Everything is dark and mysterious. Time is standing still in this picture. But something important is about to happen. What could it be?

Will the snail stretch out and touch the receiver?

Will the water drop onto the sharp razor blade?

Will the blade then slice through the smooth surface of the fried egg on the right?

When Dalí painted this picture it was peacetime in Europe, but war was just around the corner. Germany had just marched into parts of Czechoslovakia. All sorts of talks were taking place and phones were ringing non stop. At an international meeting in Munich a way to keep the peace was found, but less than a year later Adolf Hitler invaded Poland and World War II began.

The Sublime Moment, 1938

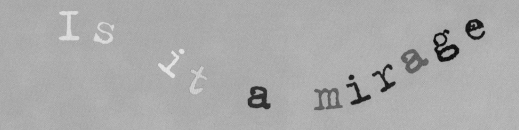

Is it a mirage

Where are we in this picture? On the beach? In the desert? In a café?
Or even at Dalí's home? There's someone with us—a boy we don't know.
Have you noticed that everything has a shadow except him? He looks
like a paper cut-out which does not really belong in the picture. Perhaps
Dalí meant us to think that we are that boy, looking at the painting.

The landscape seems like a scene from a dream. The boats, for example,
look very real, but at the same time they look quite strange because the
sea has disappeared. Things are not what they seem and can turn into
something else. In this picture, most of what Dalí painted was well-known
to him—the beach near his home, a table from the Café El Casino in
Cadaques and the kitchen floor of his house in nearby Port Lligat. The
tiles had just been laid when Dalí painted this picture.

But where did the camel come from?

Perhaps from the cigarette packet
which is lying at the boy's feet.

Sun Table, 1936

Lobster Telephone, 1936

Why not use a lobster as a telephone receiver? After all, they are nearly the same shape. Dalí loved changing ordinary things into something really surprising. He got very bored if everything just carried on as usual. Just for a change, Dalí would have thought it funny being served a grilled telephone in a restaurant instead of a lobster!

14

New fashions

*Gala wearing the
Shoe Hat*, around 1936

Salvador Dalí was very attracted to shoes. He told
the story of how, as a small boy, he secretly stole
his teacher's slipper and used it as a hat. I wonder
if he looked as elegant as his wife Gala in this
photograph. But this Shoe Hat was made in Elsa
Schiaparelli's studio. She was one of the most
popular fashion designers of the day. Of course it
was Salvador Dalí who gave her the idea for the hat
and also for the lobster dress. The lobster looks as if
it is being served on a plate decorated with parsley.
Apparently Elsa Schiaparelli only just managed to
stop Dalí garnishing the dress with real mayonnaise.

Lobster Dress, 1937

15

The lips sofa

What an elegant sofa—just perfect if you want something a bit different! But if you like unusual designs like this, be warned: the lipstick red sofa is not cheap! Dalí got the idea for this inviting piece of furniture while he was sitting on an uncomfortable rock at Cape Creus. The sofa looks like the mouth of the well-known American actress Mae West who was most famous in the 1930s.

Dalí dreamt of making a set of rooms in which the furniture and walls—when seen from a certain position—would look like Mae West. Later he made his dream come true in his museum in Figueras where he designed a 'portrait' of the actress which you could live in. A red sofa can be seen there, too.

16

Mae West
Lips Sofa, 1937

Face of Mae West, 1934/35

How can any picture be more than just one picture?

Pictures can change while you are looking at them! Dalí was mad about the idea that one thing can actually be two at the same time, and so he particularly liked to paint pictures that could be confusing.

Is this a painting of a boy crouching at the water's edge? Or is it a hand holding a bulb, just like the hand in the foreground?

A narcissus is growing out of the egg held by the hand on the right. According to Greek legend, Narcissus was the name of a handsome young man who was so beautiful that everyone fell in love with him. But he sent them all on their way. As a punishment, Narcissus was made to fall in love with his own reflection in a pool of clear water and so he suffered like the others. When he realised that he would never be able to hold, kiss or love himself, he stabbed himself to death. A narcissus sprouted on the very same spot where his blood fell. But even in the world of the dead, Narcissus could not take his eyes off his own reflection in the Styx, the river that runs through the underworld.

Dalí was also very self-centred. As a child he was spoilt by his parents because their first child, who was also called Salvador, had died when he was just two years old. Dalí recognised himself in the figure of Narcissus.

The Metamorphosis of Narcissus, 1937

There is another hand holding an egg hidden in
this picture—but only the finger tips can be seen.
Can you spot it?

The never-ending puzzle

20

In this picture Dalí has had great fun making one thing look like another. What has he hidden between the rocks of Cape Creus? It probably won't take you long to find Gala wearing a scarf on her head on the very right-hand edge of the picture, but otherwise nothing is quite how it seems. You will have to look very carefully to puzzle it all out. It's not easy at all because one thing can be several things at the same time! There are at least six different pictures hidden in this painting.

The Endless Enigma, 1938

If you can't work it out for yourself you can look at the sketches Dalí
made before painting the picture. He made a drawing of every hidden
figure and object so that it would all fit together perfectly. The face,
which can turn into both a seated woman seen from behind and a
bowl of fruit, looks like Dalí's old friend Federico García Lorca, the
Spanish poet who had died two years earlier in the Spanish Civil War.

Strange faces

Dalí got the idea for this painting when he was looking through a pile of papers for an address. He suddenly came across a picture of a face which looked as if it had been painted by Pablo Picasso. Dalí himself had been thinking quite a lot about Picasso's art at that time. But when Dalí looked at the face more closely, he saw that it wasn't a face at all. It was actually a postcard, a photograph of an African village. If you turn it on its side, you can see a face—the hut becomes a puffed out cheek; the nose is easy to find as is the neck at the bottom of the picture.

Just turn it around!

Paranoid Faces, **1931**

22

Head of a Woman Having the Form of a Battle, 1936

You don't need to turn this picture around to see that this is a face. Dalí has painted soldiers and horses in battle which also make up the face of a woman taking up the whole page! (She is looking down slightly; her eye is formed by the horse and rider in the middle, her nose outlined by the woman a bit below them just to the right). He borrowed these figures from the painter Leonardo da Vinci. Dalí was fascinated to learn that more than five hundred years ago this great Italian artist had suggested something that could well have come from Dalí himself. Leonardo had told his students to take a sponge, soak it in paint and throw it at a wall. The marks made by the sponge create unexpected pictures. Dalí said that when he was a schoolboy he would often stare at the dirty classroom ceiling. In his imagination, the big brown marks would turn into clouds and whole pictures appeared before his eyes.

23

Giuseppe Arcimboldo:
Winter, 1573

Painting like the Old Masters

Salvador Dalí also admired Leonardo and other Old Masters for the careful way they painted. From them Salvador learnt how to show every last detail and how to paint light and shade. This very clear style makes Dalí's pictures of dreams and the subconscious all the more surprising. Even today there are many people who admire Dalí for his great painting skills—skills he was always perfecting. In his book, *Fifty Magical Secrets*, Dalí tells us his secret paint recipes and how to use different sorts of brushes.

Piero della Francesca: *Battista Sforza and Federico da Montefeltro*, around 1465

Portrait of Mrs. Isabel Styler-Tas, 1945

One day a rich lady asked Dalí to paint her portrait and he decided to look at the paintings of the Old Masters to get some ideas. Dalí's picture looks a bit like the portraits of the Duke and Duchess of Urbino, painted around the middle of the fifteenth century by one of Leonardo's fellow Italians, Piero della Francesca. But who is the person opposite this lady? Is it the lady herself or another part of herself? It certainly could be her, if you look at the outlines, but otherwise she is made of rock and trees. This was not a new idea either. Four hundred years earlier the painter Giuseppe Arcimboldo loved painting pictures like this, making faces out of trees, rocks, fruit or animals.

Dalí and his 'dollar moustache' . . .

. . . and among his 'melting' clocks

Dalí the superstar

When it came to putting himself in the limelight, Dalí always had unusual ideas that attracted the attention of the newspapers and the public. He was very clever at presenting himself as an artistic genius. His wife Gala helped him to do this. Soon Dalí was earning a lot of money through his art and he lived a life of luxury with the rich, famous and beautiful. His fellow painters, who also belonged to the Surrealists, got more and more annoyed because Dalí was always pushing himself into the centre of attention. Their leader, André Breton, played around with the letters in Salvador Dalí's name and came up with the words 'avida dollars'—which in Spanish actually exists and means 'greedy for dollars'!

As these photographs show, Dalí loved posing for the cameras.
But who knows what he really looked like?

Salvador Dalí ...

... with Gala in
her Paris flat

... as Father Christmas with Gala,
signing his *Diary of a Genius*

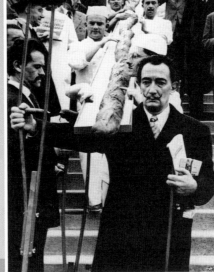

... at a trade fair
in Paris with his loaf
of white bread which
measured twelve
metres long

27

... as the Mona Lisa

... on the cover of Time

... next to his 'soft self-portrait'

Salvador Dalí wrote a book about his life called The Secret Life of Salvador Dalí. He didn't always keep to the truth because he wanted to present himself as a genius surrounded by legends. His ancestors were not pirates, as he said they were, but there may really has been a bit of Arabic blood in his veins.

Salvador Felipe Jacinto Dalí y Domenech was born on 11 May, 1904 in Figueras (Catalonian: Figueres) in Catalonia. He had his first drawing lessons at secondary school and, at the age of fourteen, was already showing his own pictures at an exhibition of local painters in the municipal theatre in Figueras. A year later he published articles about painters he admired, including Leonardo da Vinci.

In 1921 Dalí went to study in Madrid and became friends with the writer Federico García Lorca and the film director Luis Buñuel. He soon attracted a lot of attention through his exhibitions but just before his final exams, Dalí was thrown out of the academy because he said that his teachers were not capable of assessing his work.

During a stay in Paris in 1929, Dalí got to know the Surrealists. A number of these artists, including the poet Paul Éluard and his wife Gala, visited him in Spain shortly afterwards. Gala and Dalí fell in love and were inseparable from then on. A year later, Dalí bought a fisherman's cottage in Port Lligat near Cadaques which he renovated so that he could live in it.

In 1934 he paid his first visit to the USA. In Paris he met Harpo Marx and, during his second visit to the USA, he planned a film with the Marx brothers but it was never actually made. In 1938 he took part in a large exhibition of Surrealist works. One of the main attractions was his 'rain taxi', a taxi where artificial rain fell from the roof. Back in New York, Dalí sold twenty-one pictures to a private collector for a huge sum of money. At the age of thirty-seven, Dalí had a big exhibition in the Museum of Modern Art in New York which travelled to eight other American cities. Dalí's fame was spread fast throughout America and in 1944 he designed a dream scene for Alfred Hitchcock's film *Spellbound*. In 1948 Dalí returned to Port Lligat. In 1974 he opened his own museum called the Teatre-Museu Dalí in Figueras. Salvador Dalí died in his hometown on 23 January, 1989, six-and-a-half years after his wife Gala.

The Surrealist movement began in Paris in the early twenties. Writers and poets of the times invented the concept 'sur-réalité' meaning 'beyond reality'. It wasn't long before they were joined by painters, sculptors and photographers. The Surrealists were interested in magic, dreams and the subconscious. They thought that it was boring and unimaginative to obey rules and be sensible.

This is why they welcomed Dalí with open arms. He invented the 'critical paranoiac' method ('paranoia' means 'insanity' or being mad). Some mentally ill people can imagine things that are not there. Dalí believed that such people are very good at drawing puzzling pictures. Dalí said that the only difference between himself and a mad person was that he himself wasn't actually mad. He looked at this sort of imagined picture 'critically' and used this in his work as a painter.